IMPRESSIONS of

CATHEDRAL
CITIES

Produced by AA Publishing
© AA Media Limited 2009

Published by AA Publishing (a trading name of AA Media Limited, whose registered
office is Fanum House, Basing View,
Basingstoke, Hampshire RG21 4EA; registered number 06112600)

ISBN: 978-0-7495-6180-2
A04091

A CIP catalogue record for this book is available from the British Library.

The contents of this book are believed correct at the time of printing. Nevertheless,
the publishers cannot be held responsible for any errors, omissions or for changes in
the details given in this book or for the consequences of any reliance on the
information provided by the same. This does not affect your statutory rights.

Colour reproduction by KDP, Kingsclere
Printed and bound in China by C & C Offset Printing Co. Ltd

Opposite: A view towards Ely Cathedral, Cambridgeshire. The tallest tower is the West Tower at 215ft (66m).

IMPRESSIONS *of*

CATHEDRAL CITIES

Picture Acknowledgements

The Automobile Association would like to thank the following photographers, companies
and picture libraries for their assistance in the preparation of this book.

Abbreviations for the picture credits are as follows: (AA) AA World Travel Library

Cover Premier/Alamy; Back Cover AA/T Mackie; Back Cover left AA/J Beazley

3 AA/T Mackie; 5 AA/S Day; 7 AA/J Beazley; 8 AA/T Mackie; 9 AA/T Mackie; 10 AA/J Tims; 11 AA/M Birkitt;
12 AA/M Alexander; 13 AA/P and G Bowater; 14 AA/P Bennett; 15 AA/R Coulam; 16 AA/J Tims; 17 AA/J
Tims; 18 AA/S Day; 19 AA/S Day; 20 AA/J Miller; 21 AA/P Brown; 22 AA/T Mackie; 23 AA/T Mackie; 24
AA/M Moody; 25 AA/M Moody; 26 AA/M Birkitt; 27 AA/C Jones; 28 AA/H Palmer; 29 AA/S Day; 30 AA/N
Setchfield; 31 AA/N Setchfield; 32 AA/ T Mackie; 33 AA/T Mackie; 34 AA/I Burgum; 35 AA/M Moody; 36
AA/J Welsh; 37 AA/J Welsh; 38 AA/M Busselle; 39 AA/J Beazley; 40 AA/S McBride; 41 AA/R Victor; 42 AA/S
Day; 43 AA/S Day; 44 AA/N Hicks; 45 AA/W Voysey; 46 AA/H Palmer; 47 AA/M Moody; 48 AA/K Paterson;
49 AA/C Jones; 50 AA/C Jones; 51 AA/N Hicks; 52 AA/N Setchfield; 53 AA/B Smith; 54 AA/T Woodcock; 55
AA/N Jenkins; 56 AA/J Smith; 57 AA/J Smith; 58 AA/S Day; 59 AA/M Moody; 60 AA/T Mackie; 61 AA/T
Mackie; 62 AA/S and O Matthews; 63 AA/J Miller; 64 AA/P Baker; 65 AA/M Busselle; 66 AA/L Whitwan; 67
AA/L Whitwan; 68 AA/M Moody; 69 AA/N Hicks; 70 AA/R Moss; 71 AA/C Jones; 72 AA/J Tims; 73 AA/J
Tims; 74 AA/J Miller; 75 AA/J Miller; 76 AA/S Day; 77 AA/H Palmer; 78 AA/N Hicks; 79 AA/J Tims; 80 AA/N
Jenkins; 81 AA/R Coulam; 82 AA/R Moss; 83 AA/C Jones; 84 AA/J Tims; 85 AA/T Mackie; 86 AA/M Moody;
87 AA/S Day; 88 AA/T Mackie; 89 AA/T Mackie; 90 AA/M Alexander; 91 AA/H Palmer; 92 AA/J Tims; 93
AA/M Moody; 94 AA/R Rainford; 95 AA/T Mackie.

Every effort has been made to trace the copyright holders, and we apologise in advance for any unintentional
omissions or errors. We would be happy to apply the corrections in any following edition of this publication.

Opposite: The fan-vaulted ceilings of Gloucester Cathedral's cloisters are the finest in Europe and date back to the 14th century.

INTRODUCTION

The link between cathedrals and city status dates from the Reformation and the founding of the English church. Officially, the term 'cathedral city' today only applies to cities with an Anglican Cathedral, although having an Anglican Cathedral is not necessarily a guarantee of cathedral city status as Bury St Edmunds and Guildford can testify. In Scotland there is no link between the presence of an Anglican Cathedral and the title of 'cathedral city' but the English definition has been applied here to allow us to include some of its beautiful cities. The technicalities are somewhat complicated but the majesty of these buildings and their cities speaks for themselves.

Fittingly, Britain's capital has perhaps its crowning glory of cathedral splendour, Christopher Wren's St Paul's Cathedral, which towers over the City of London, Britain's second-smallest official city. This majestic domed creation is the fourth cathedral to occupy this Thameside site, its predecessor having been destroyed in London's Great Fire of 1666.

The City of London is beaten to the title of Britain's smallest city by St David's in southwest Wales which has a population of just under 2,000. The city is tucked away on the Pembrokeshire peninsula and the cathedral itself is hidden in a valley, yet its importance should not be underestimated. Dating from the 6th century and housing the remains of St David, the site has long been a major pilgrimage destination and it is said that two visits to St David's equals one to Rome.

Perhaps surprisingly, one of the oldest cities in England is Coventry, although tragically much of its history, including its cathedral was destroyed during the heavy bombing it sustained in the Second World War. Today, Basil Spence's striking modern cathedral has taken its place, with the atmospheric ruins of the old cathedral left as a garden of remembrance in its grounds.

The city of Liverpool takes the concept of two cathedrals one step further, boasting two complete cathedrals, an Anglican and a Roman Catholic one. Standing at either end of the significantly named Hope Street, the two cathedrals dominate the city skyline. The Anglican cathedral is particularly imposing and claims the title of largest cathedral in Britain and the fifth largest in the world.

Another cathedral famous for its size is York Minster, the largest Gothic cathedral in northern Europe. It was commissioned by Archbishop Walter de Gray who wanted a church as big and as grand as Canterbury Cathedral. If it was Gothic splendour he was aiming for, he certainly achieved his aim.

Three of England's cathedrals, Durham, Canterbury and Bath, are within World Heritage Sites and many others including Winchester, Salisbury and Ely attract visitors from all over the world. The cities they are located in are no less fascinating – all are concentrated pockets of history, yet each with its own character and atmosphere.

Opposite: Durham's 14th-century castle and its Norman cathedral were together inscribed as one of Britain's first World Heritage Sites.

Lincoln Cathedral is one of the finest medieval buildings in Europe and towers over the city of Lincoln.
Opposite: Around seventy per cent of Lincoln Cathedral's beautiful stained glass windows are original.

A hollyhock flower in Salisbury's Cathedral Close with the cathedral spire, the tallest in Britain, in the background.

It is claimed that the west tower of Ely Cathedral is visible from almost every church in the diocese.

Glasgow Cathedral with its 13th-century tower, is the city's oldest building.

Opposite: In Glasgow's Cathedral Square, decorative wrought-iron work on the lamp posts reflects the city's coat-of-arms.

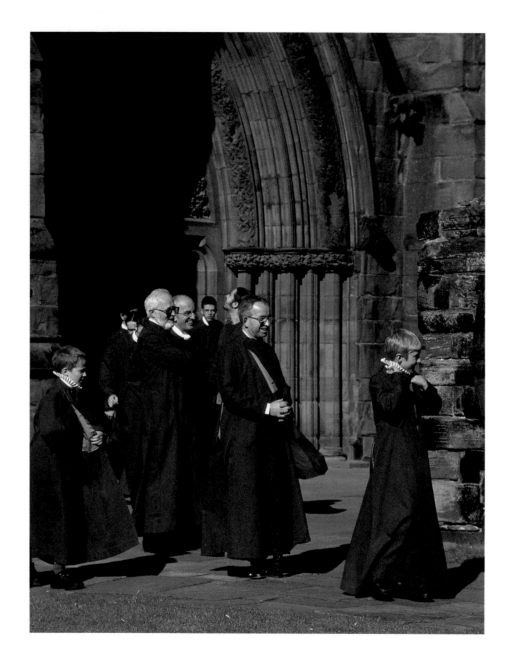

Carlisle Cathedral was founded in 1133 and has a proud choral tradition going back 900 years.

Carlisle is situated just a few miles from the Scottish border but, despite a turbulent history, its cathedral has survived.

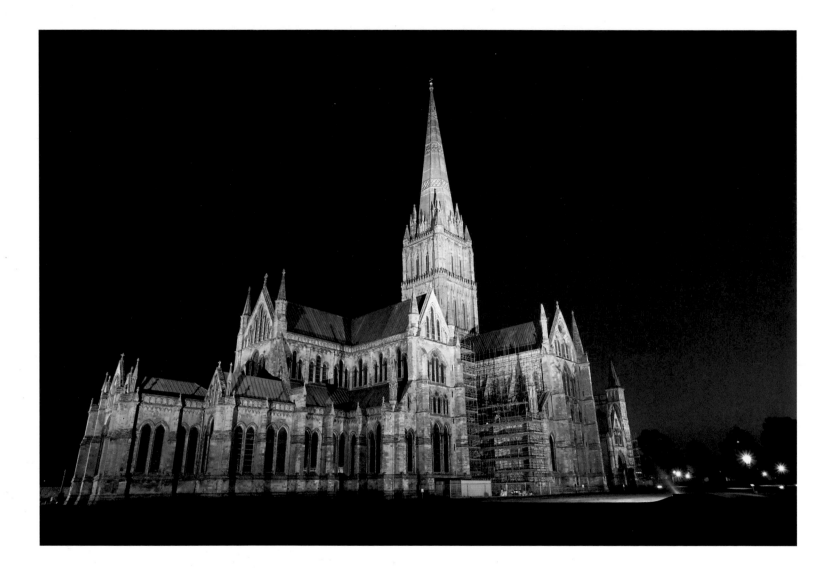

*Salisbury Cathedral is unique amongst medieval English cathedrals, in that
it was built within one century with no substantial later additions.
Opposite: The cathedral is Gothic in style and has 67 statues on its west front.*

An art deco door handle inside the 20th-century Anglican Cathedral in Liverpool.

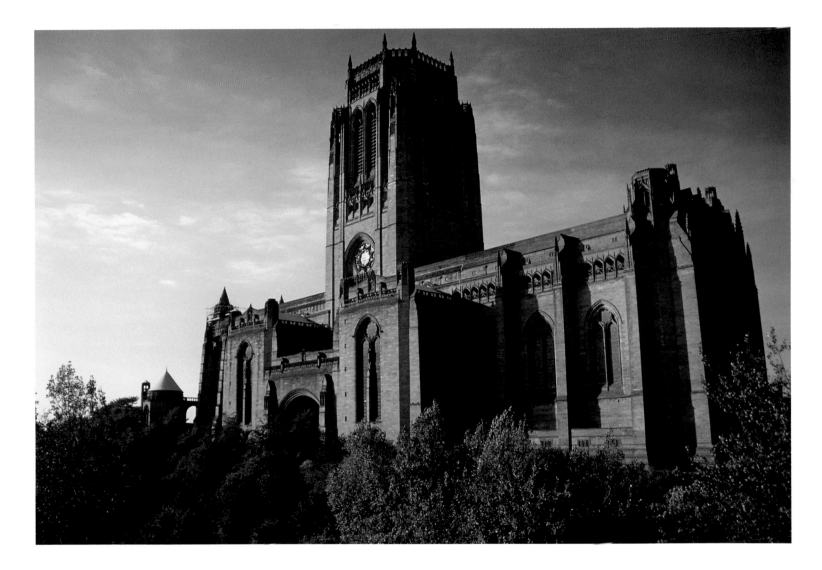

The Cathedral Church of Christ, Liverpool, has the highest and heaviest peel of church bells in the world.

The building of the present cathedral in Chichester was begun in 1076 under Bishop Stigand.
Opposite: Elsewhere in the town, a colourful hanging basket compliments the painted exterior of an antiques shop.

A statue of Alfred Lord Tennyson stands outside Lincoln Cathedral.
The famous poet was born at Somersby in Lincolnshire in 1809.
Opposite: The interior of Lincoln Cathedral features one of the finest cathedral organs in the country.

The building of Worcester Cathedral was hampered by the collapse of the central tower in 1175 and a fire in 1203.

On a clear day, the top of Worcester Cathedral's tower offers spectacular views across the city centre, the River Severn and the Malvern Hills.

Close-up of Peterborough Cathedral, Cambridgeshire, with its ornate archways. The present building was begun in 1118 and consecrated in 1238, with a number of additions since then.

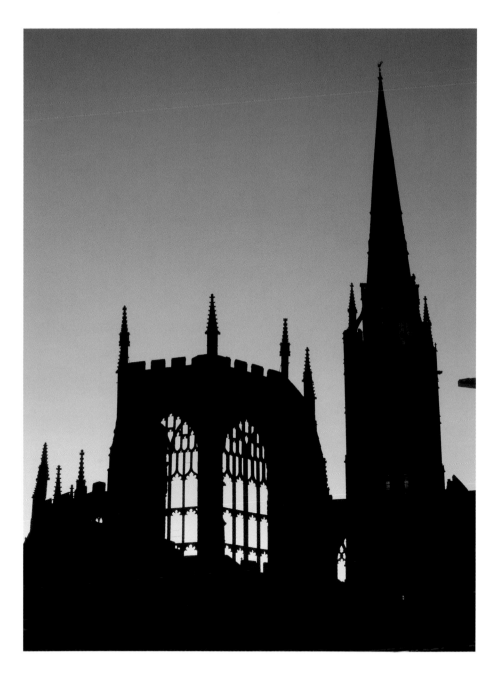

Dusk at the ruins of St Michael's Cathedral, Coventry, which became a victim of the Blitz on the night of 14th November 1940.

The west front of Gloucester Cathedral which was remodelled in the 15th century.

Light streams through the dome of the mid 20th-century Roman Catholic Cathedral of Christ the King, Liverpool. The cathedral's unusual design was the result of a worldwide design competition which was won by Sir Frederick Gibberd.

Rochester Castle boasts the largest Norman keep in the country. It was built by William de Corbeil, Archbishop of Canterbury.

Despite having the second oldest cathedral in England, Rochester lost its official city status in 2002 due to an administrative error four years earlier.

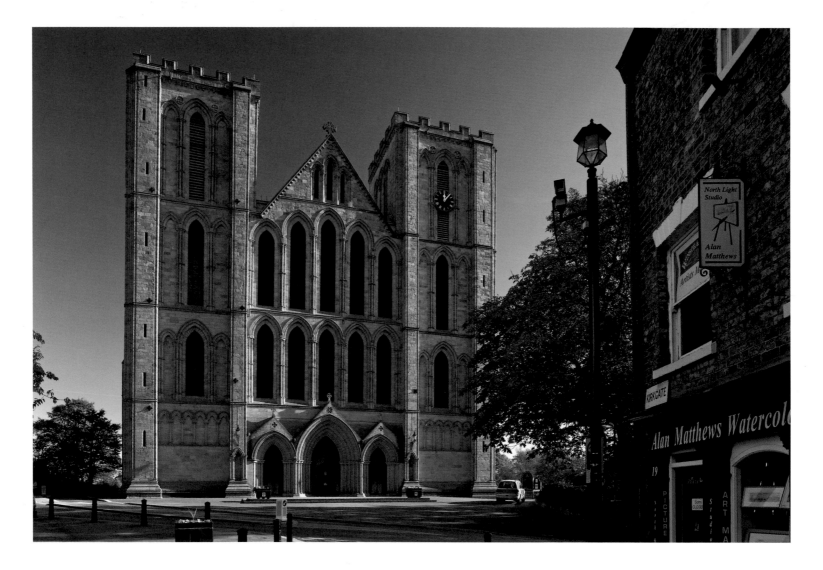

The facade of Ripon Cathedral with parts dating from the 13th century.

Opposite: Ripon Cathedral is one of England's smaller cathedrals. It was elevated to cathedral status in 1836.

St David's Cathedral in the Pembrokeshire Coast National Park dates from the 12th century.
St David, the Patron Saint of Wales, founded a monastery on this site in around AD 589.

Views of Winchester and its Cathedral Church, so called because it houses the throne (or 'cathedra') of the Bishop of Winchester.

It has its origins in the seventh century when a Christian church was first built on the site.

Quoinian's Lane in the cathedral city of Lichfield is characterised by its timber-framed 18th-century houses.

Opposite: House-lined Westgate leading to the 13th-century west front of Lichfield Cathedral, which is covered in 19th-century statues.

Detail of some of the crests on an interior wall of Canterbury Cathedral. The cathedral is perhaps most famous as the site of Archbishop Thomas Becket's murder in 1170.

Durham Cathedral is built on a peninsula of land created by a loop in the River Wear. The west end towers over a precipitous gorge.

St Paul's Cathedral, London was designed by Sir Christopher Wren.
Its foundation stone was laid in 1675 and the building was completed in 1710.
Today the Millennium Bridge leads visitors to it over the River Thames.

Detail of the roof above the choir at Winchester Cathedral.
Opposite: In the North aisle of Winchester Cathedral's crypt stands Antony Gormley's sculpture, 'Sound II'.
Made of lead, it shows a person seeing a reflection of their soul in a bowl of water.

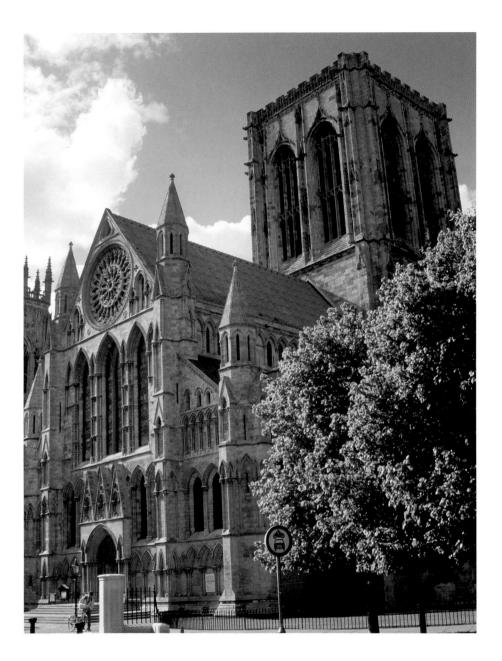

The west facade and a tower of the medieval Minster at York. New stonework around the west door was completed in 1998.

Opposite: Ancient gateway on Cathedral Close, Exeter.

Worcester's Guildhall was designed by Thomas White, a pupil of Sir Christopher Wren. He was poorly paid for his work and died in poverty in 1738. He bestowed the money he was owed on Worcester Royal Infirmary but it was not paid until 15 years after his death.

Worcester Cathedral is famous for its beautiful location on the banks of the River Severn.

A statue of Walter Francis, 5th Duke of Buccleuch, stands behind St Giles' Cathedral in Parliament Square, Edinburgh.

Opposite: Coventry's new St Michael's Cathedral can be seen here at dusk through the ruins of its predecessor. The decision to build a new cathedral was taken the very morning after the bombings that destroyed the old one, as a symbol of faith in humanity and peace in the future.

Carving detail on Exeter Cathedral, Devon.

The North tower of Exeter Cathedral. The cathedral took a direct hit in the Blitz of 1942 but both towers have since been completely restored.

The Cupola of St Paul's Cathedral is an iconic feature of the London skyline. Visitors can climb to the Golden Gallery for a bird's eye view of the city or admire the elaborate mosaics on the interior. The cupola is also famous for its Whispering Gallery, where the acoustics of the curved surface mean that a whispered phrase can be heard at any point around the circular walkway inside the dome.

A Gothic sanctuary knocker belonging to Durham Cathedral.

Opposite: The screen, organ and pendulum in St David's Cathedral, Pembrokeshire Coast National Park.

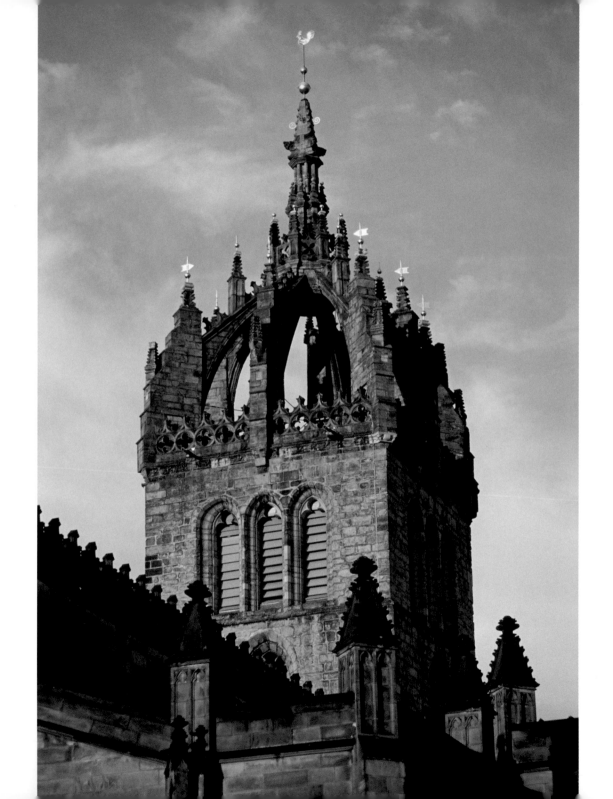

Edinburgh Castle's Royal Apartments and Half Moon Battery.

Opposite: The crown spire of St Giles' Cathedral, Edinburgh, which stands on Edinburgh's Royal Mile between Edinburgh Castle and the Palace of Holyroodhouse.

A swan on the river in Salisbury, Wiltshire, with the spire of the cathedral in the background.

The Butter Cross in Winchester, Hampshire, is thought to date from the early 15th century. It was originally used by countrymen to sell produce, hence its name.

Intricately decorated on both the inside and the outside, Ely Cathedral is a magnificent Norman cathedral that attracts visitors from all over the world. The shrine of its founder, St. Etheldreda, brought vast numbers of medieval pilgrims to this site until its destruction in 1541. Today, a slate in the cathedral marks the spot where it stood.

Close up detail of the painted wooden ceiling of the Nave roof in Peterborough Cathedral.

View of Chichester Cathedral. With Roman walls, a medieval heart and a cathedral that dominates the area, Chichester has far more for visitors than you would expect for a city of its size.

The timber-framed Conquest House stands decorated with colourful hanging baskets of flowers in the streets of Canterbury. Opposite: The entrance gate of Canterbury Cathedral. The figure of Christ seen in the centre is a modern replacement for a figure destroyed during the Civil War.

A round window of Norwich School Chapel at Norwich Cathedral, Norfolk.

Norwich Cathedral's foundation stone was laid by Bishop Herbert de Losinga in 1096.

Views from the top of the tower of Worcester Cathedral over the River Severn.

A medieval building on Cathedral Close, Exeter.

Truro Cathedral is built on the site of the former Parish Church of St Mary. The cathedral architect John Loughborough Pearson kept the South Aisle of the old Parish Church and incorporated it into his design for the cathedral, creating a church within a church.
Opposite: The interior of 19th-century Truro Cathedral is vaulted throughout and built of local granite and stone.

Cathedral Cloisters, Wells. Excavated foundations here show remains of the first church built on this site in AD *705.*

Detail of the west facade of Wells Cathedral. The facade has niches for more than 500 figure sculptures, many of them larger than lifesize.

Spire of Chichester Cathedral against a blue sky. The cathedral was consecrated in 1108.

Pink hydrangea growing beside a wall in historic Chichester.

St Oswald's Priory and the tower of Gloucester Cathedral. The priory was founded in about AD 890 by the daughter of Alfred the Great. Opposite: Gloucester's Historic Docks, home to Britain's most inland port.

A view of the north side of Exeter Cathedral. It is considered the finest surviving example of Decorated Gothic,
a form of architecture that flourished in England from 1270 to 1369.

Salisbury Cathedral and the Walking Madonna statue by Dame Elisabeth Frink, which can be found on the West Walk.

Organ pipes in St David's Cathedral, Pembrokeshire Coast National Park. The organ was built by Henry Willis in 1883 and rebuilt in 1953 when it was given a new case by the architect Alban Caroe.

Opposite: Wispy cirrus clouds float above the roof of Carlisle Cathedral. The cathedral's stained glass dates from the 14th to the 20th centuries.

A close view of a flying buttress on Truro Cathedral. The cathedral was built by the Victorians in the medieval Gothic style.

Truro competed with Bodmin and St Germains to be chosen as the site for the proposed cathedral for the Cornish See.

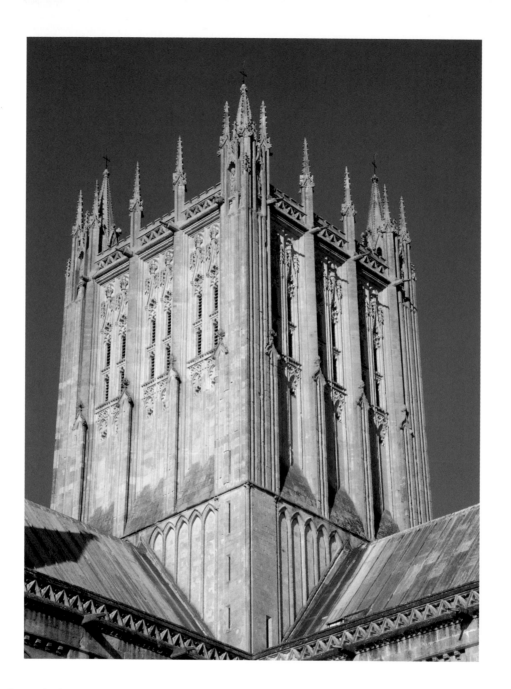

The current Wells Cathedral building was begun in 1180 and has survived eight centuries with the buildings around it intact.

Looking up to the nave ceiling, 105ft (32m) above the floor of Ely Cathedral.

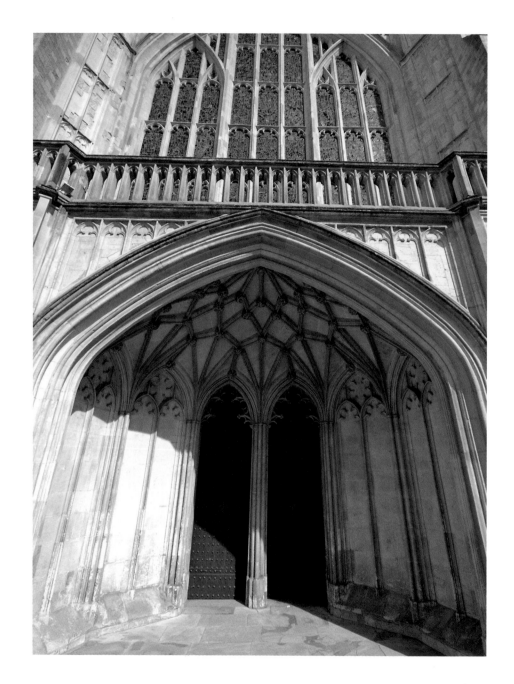

Red doors of Winchester Cathedral. The original structure of the cathedral was built on swamp land over 1,000 years ago and was only saved from sinking by the ingenuity of two Edwardian engineers.

The east end of Winchester Cathedral was greatly extended during the 13th century to include the Retrochoir.

Steep Hill in Lincoln links the modern shopping area of Lincoln with the historic area at the top of the hill.

The height of the central tower of Lincoln Cathedral was raised in the 14th century and topped with a lead-covered spire,
making the cathedral the tallest building in Europe at that time.

Glasgow Cathedral. The first stone building on this site was consecrated in about 1136 in the presence of King David I and his Court.

Houses viewed across River Wye at Hereford. The river runs through the old city and past the cathedral grounds.

Winchester town clock is on the old Guildhall. It was gifted to the city by its members of Parliament to commemorate the visit of the Queen in 1713.

Opposite: The west facade of Wells Cathedral was built between 1209 and 1250. It is 150ft (45.7m) wide – exactly twice the width of the Nave.

The Wye Bridge in Hereford was first built in 1490 and widened in 1826. It was preceded by an even older bridge of wood built in 1120. Hereford Cathedral can been seen behind it.

The Octagon is the site of the principal altar in Ely Cathedral. A series of medieval carvings on either side of the arches of the main pillars around the Octagon are among the few to have survived the Reformation.

INDEX